Cat Nap

Written by Inbali Iserles

Illustrated by Yana Kozak

Collins

Cat naps.

Cat can not nap.

Nap on a sack.

Cat can not nap.

Nap on a mat.

The dog taps. Cat can not nap.

Nap on a cot.

The cot tips! Cat can not nap.

Kam sits. Kam pats.

Kam naps.

Cat naps!

/n/

14

/g/

15

Review: After reading

Use your assessment from hearing the children read to choose any GPCs, words or tricky words that need additional practice.

Read 1: Decoding

- Read page 2 and talk about the sound words **pit pat**. Ask: What is making the sound? (*the rain*)
- Read pages 4 and 5. Ask the children to point to the letter or letters that make each /c/ sound. (*ck, c*) Ask the children to read page 10. Encourage them to blend in their heads, silently, before reading the words aloud. Ask: Can you find the same /c/ sound on page 10 but spelled differently? (*K – Kam*)
- Look at the "I spy sounds" pages (14–15). Point to the nest, and say "nest", emphasising the /n/ sound. Ask the children to find items in the picture that start with the /n/ sound. (e.g. *newspaper, necklace, nap, nose*) Repeat for the /g/ sound. (e.g. *goose, grapes, guitar, glasses*)

Read 2: Prosody

- Read pages 8 and 9, modelling using a storyteller's voice to create excitement.
- Discuss the change of tone you used when reading the first sentence on page 9. Ask: Why did I use a surprised tone? (*to show that something suddenly happened – the cot tipped over*)
- Encourage the children to experiment with tone and emphasis as they read the second sentence. Ask: Do you want this sentence to sound funny or serious? Why? (e.g. *funny because the cat has been woken up again*)

Read 3: Comprehension

- Discuss any times the children have been woken up. Ask: What woke you up? How did you feel?
- Talk about the different places the cat tried to sleep. (*garden, sack, mat, cot*) What woke the cat? (*rain, a clock alarm, the dog tapping, the dog knocking over the cot*) Ask: Do you think the cat will be able to nap on Kam's lap? Why? (e.g. *yes, because it will be cosy and quiet, and Kam will keep the dog away*)